Stringtastic
BOOK 1: CELLO

Mark Wilson and Paul Wood
With illustrations by Sarah-Leigh Wills

For online backing tracks scan the QR code
or go to fabermusic.com/audio

FABER *ff* MUSIC

Contents

All music and lyrics by Mark Wilson and Paul Wood unless otherwise stated.

The rights of Mark Wilson and Paul Wood to be identified as the joint authors of this work, and of Sarah-Leigh Wills to be identified as the creator of page illustrations in this work, have been asserted in accordance with the Copyright, Designs and Patents Act, 1988.

© 2022 by Faber Music Ltd
First published by Faber Music Ltd
Bloomsbury House, 74–77 Great Russell Street, London WC1B 3DA
Music processed by Donald Thomson
Cover design by WattGenius Creative
Page design by Chloë Alexander
Page illustrations by Sarah-Leigh Wills
Printed in England by Caligraving Ltd
All rights reserved

ISBN10: 0-571-54257-3
EAN13: 978-0-571-54257-4

To buy Faber Music publications or to find out about the full range of titles available please contact your local music retailer or Faber Music sales enquiries:

Faber Music Ltd, Burnt Mill, Elizabeth Way, Harlow CM20 2HX
Tel: +44 (0) 1279 82 89 82
fabermusic.com

Learn as you play through the world of *Stringtastic!*

Stringtastic Book 1 is an exciting collection of fun new compositions covering
a wide range of styles. These pieces are progressively presented, taking the player
on a journey from the D major scale through to Grade 1 (Early Elementary) level.
No more than one technique is introduced at a time and space is given for consolidation.

These books have been designed for maximum flexibility:

- *Stringtastic Book 1* for violin, viola, cello and double bass is fully integrated to
  work together in any combination — ideal for use in individual lessons as well as
  group lessons and string orchestras.

- Many tunes have fun lyrics to sing, helping to develop a strong sense of pitch and rhythm.
  Learners can try writing their own lyrics, too!

- Dynamics are given throughout, but players are encouraged to add their own once a
  confident sound has been developed. Where there are lyrics, dynamics have consistently
  been placed below the lyric line and apply to both parts in the duets.

- Fingering is left to the discretion of the teacher.

- While there are 57 pieces in total, eight of these are equal-level duets, both accompanied
  and unaccompanied; here players are encouraged to learn both parts.

- Every tune has a fun backing track to play along to, as well as a piano-only
  backing track for practice:

 Scan the QR code or go to fabermusic.com/audio to download the tracks.

1. Time for C!

Happily ♩ = 80—112
Count 2 bars

Time for C, then it's B, A and B and then it's C!

f

Next to C is a B, A and B and then it's C!

Nice and stea - dy, play with me.

This is C, this is B, A and B and then it's C!

2. Deep feelings

Flowing ♩ = 72
Count 2 bars

p

rit.

3. Gee up!

Simply ♩ = 84—120

Count 2 bars

There's noth-ing quite like the sound of low notes, come on and let us sing!

Make sure your bow arm is at the right height, so our string can ring!

C, C, B, A, A, B, C, C, B, A, B, A, G, G!

You'll have such fun play-ing low notes like me, we make a rich, warm sound.

Smile as you play all us love-ly low notes; with a sound so round!

4. Welly Bob shuffle

Give it welly! ♩ = 92—120

Count 4 bars

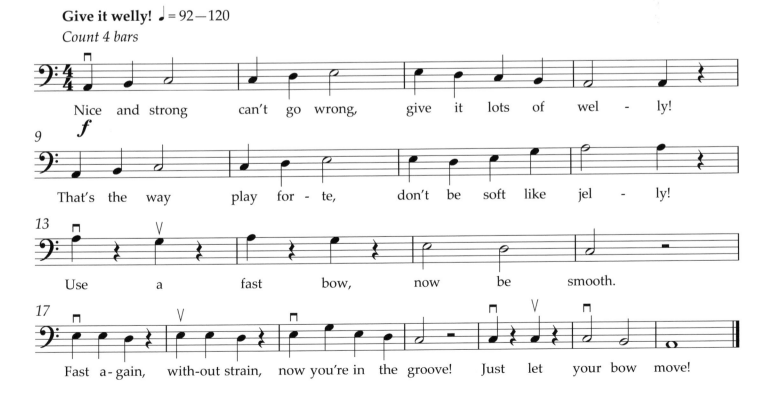

Nice and strong can't go wrong, give it lots of wel - ly!

That's the way play for - te, don't be soft like jel - ly!

Use a fast bow, now be smooth.

Fast a-gain, with-out strain, now you're in the groove! Just let your bow move!

5. Boogie bow

With energy ♩ = 112 – 138

Count 4 bars

6. C air

Buoyant ♩ = 72
Count 2 bars

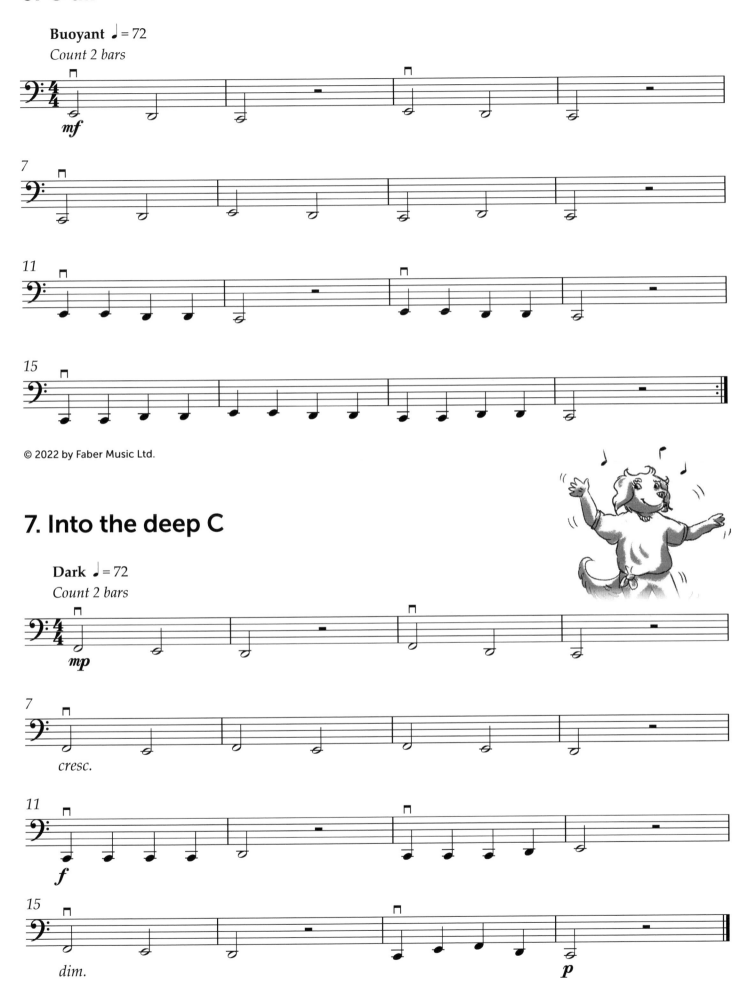

7. Into the deep C

Dark ♩ = 72
Count 2 bars

8. Bassers and chasers

Adventurous ♩ = 108—132

Count 1 bar

We can play a D and E,

f

we can play an E and D!

We can al - so play a note called F, so play an F, then E and D.

These are notes C can play.

p

pizz.

They sound ve - ry low, but they sound great, so let the mu - sic flow to - day. Yay!

f

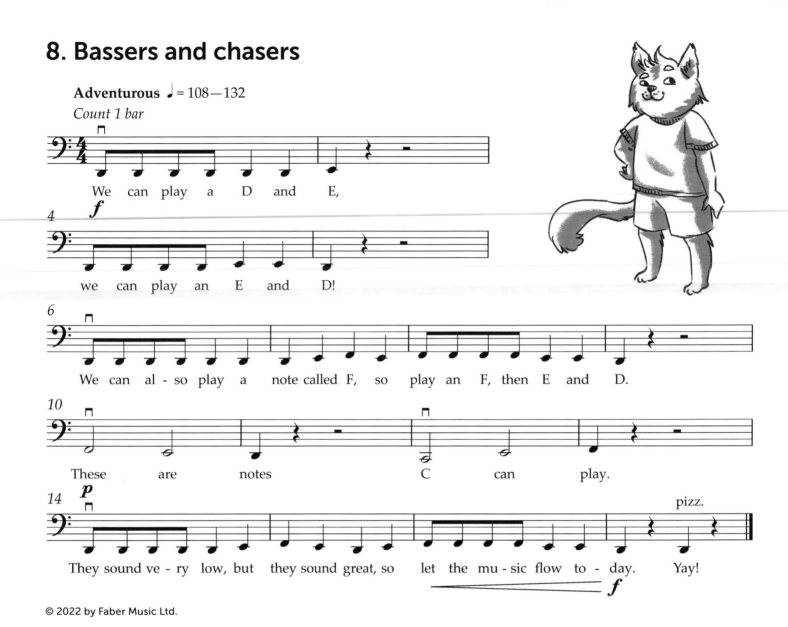

9. City of dust

Far away ♩ = 72

Count 2 bars

p

mf

f

p

10. Listen

11. Flowing downstream

12. Happy and free

13. Be a butterfly

Flighty ♩ = 100
Count 2 bars

Be   a   but - ter - fly,   rea - dy   to   take   off.

mf

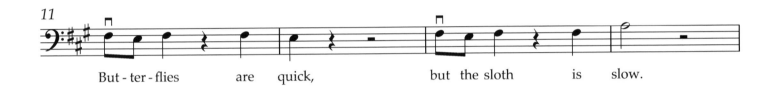

Be   a   but - ter - fly,   or   you   could   be   a   sloth!

But - ter - flies   are   quick,   but the sloth   is   slow.

But - ter - flies,   they spread their wings and,   flut - ter - ing,   they   go.   So,

be   a   but - ter - fly,   rea - dy   to   take   flight.

Why   not   be a moth   and   fly   off   in   the   night?

14. When the world has gone to sleep

Like a hymn ♩ = 76—92

Count 2 bars

When the world has gone to sleep, all the peo-ple count-ing sheep,
I'm a-wake in my bed, writ-ing mu-sic in my head.
Then, at last, sleep draws near and the tunes dis-ap-pear.
When I wake they've flown a-way, chased off by the break of day.
Mu-sic where have you gone? You have van-ished with the dawn.

15. A hint of jasmine

Gently swaying ♩ = 66—88

Count 2 bars

16. Smoothly does it

17. Blue sky

18. Sometimes

19. Sticky toffee pudding

Enthusiastically ♩ = 60—76

Count 2 bars

Sti - cky tof - fee pud - ding, pep - pe - ro - ni piz - za,

f

stacked up on my plate, that does look yum - my.

Shep - herd's pie and cus - tard, broc - co - li and choc - 'late,

topped off with some rhu - barb in my tum - my.

When my plate is clean my bel - ly starts to rum - ble,

p

I can hear it grum - ble, I don't know why!

Run - ning from the ta - ble, head - ing for the bath - room,

f

hop - ing I'm in time 'cause I FEEL SICK!

20. Clever cat

With *feline!* ♩ = 66 — 84

Count 2 bars

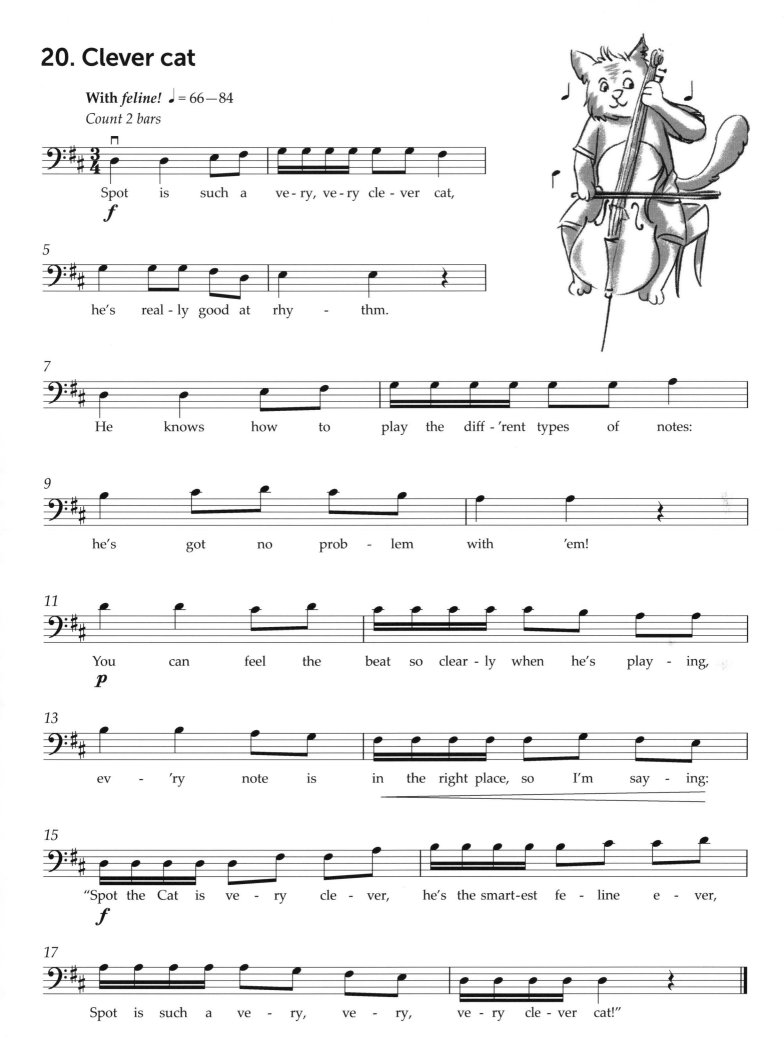

Spot is such a ve-ry, ve-ry cle-ver cat,

f

he's real-ly good at rhy - thm.

He knows how to play the diff -'rent types of notes:

he's got no prob - lem with 'em!

You can feel the beat so clear-ly when he's play-ing,

p

ev -'ry note is in the right place, so I'm say-ing:

"Spot the Cat is ve - ry cle - ver, he's the smart-est fe - line e - ver,

f

Spot is such a ve-ry, ve-ry, ve-ry cle - ver cat!"

21. Come and play with us

Hip ♩ = 96—112

Count 2 bars

Spot and Dot - ty clap and sing, they point and then they say all the

names and lengths of notes and that's when Spot and Dot - ty play! Let us

count and lis - ten, bow and fin - ger, think and then dis - cuss, 'cause we're

hip and tren - dy, cool and hap - py, come and play with us! Yeah!

22. Dotty's dotted notes

Rhythmically ♩ = 76—88

Count 2 bars

Look at Dot - ty danc-ing to the rhy-thm of our dot - ty dot - ted notes!

Spot just loves to lis - ten to the sound we make as through the air it floats.

Dot - ted notes are real - ly ea - sy, I'm sure you'll a - gree.

1, 2, 3, 4, 1 & 2 & 3 & 4 & 1 (2) & 3 (4) & 1 (2, off).

23. Playtime

Happily ♩ = 76—88

Count 2 bars

Spin and jump and feel the rhy-thm of the mu - sic.

Dance and twirl and move your bo - dy to the beat.

Laugh and smile and fill the world with joy - ful sing - ing.

Play and sway and lis-ten to the love - ly sound you

make! So come on, let's play!

24. Quiver of eighths

Flighty ♩. = 54—76

Count 2 bars

25. Higgledy-piggledy

Cool ♩. = 66—76

Count 2 bars

Hig - gle - dy - pig - gle - dy, what can

Spot likes 6 8

I do to work this thing out?

'cause he's cool!

Prac - tice and prac - tice and prac - tice, prac - tice will sort it all out. So,

He can count it: he's no fool!

1 2 3, 4 5 6. That's right: 1 2 3, 4 5 6. THAT'S RIGHT!

1 2 3, 4 5 6. That's right: 1 2 3, 4 5 6. THAT'S RIGHT!

Hig - gle - dy - pig - gle - dy, sort - ed! Was - n't so hard af - ter all! Yeah!

6 8's ea - sy and it's cool! Yeah!

26. Ducks on a pond

Pic-ture a pond where some ducks stay, look-ing se-rene, glid-ing all day.

Their lit-tle feet pad-dle a-way, danc-ing their own un-der-wa-ter bal-let.

The fin-gers of your left hand should work just like ducks' bu-sy feet.

Mean-while, your bow glides on the string, mak-ing a sound smooth and sweet!

27. Hide-and-seek

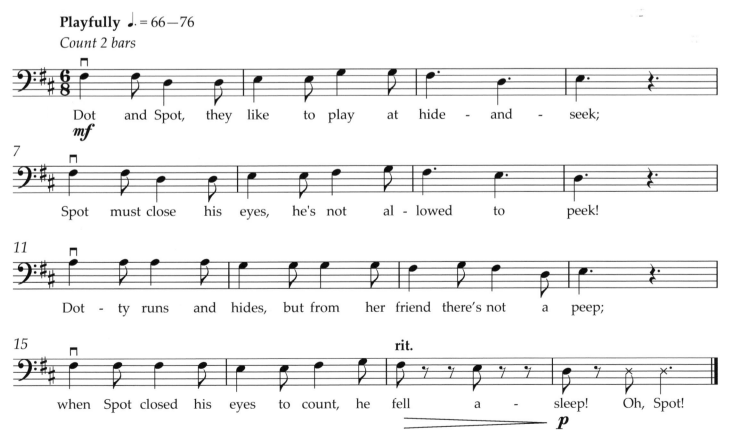

Dot and Spot, they like to play at hide - and - seek;

Spot must close his eyes, he's not al - lowed to peek!

Dot - ty runs and hides, but from her friend there's not a peep;

when Spot closed his eyes to count, he fell a - sleep! Oh, Spot!

28. Jig together

With lift ♩. = 63—80

29. Dark forest

Darkly ♩ = 76

Count 2 bars

30. Four great friends

Cosily ♩ = 88

Count 2 bars

Four great friends come to play,

f

11

E is with F, G, A.

31. Bullfrog rant

With drive ♩ = 84—100

I am a great big frog, I'm danc-ing on a log, you'll find me in a bog. Dance with me!

f

5

Hey, can you feel the beat? Stay light u-pon your feet. Come, dance with me and eat flies all day!

9

Long and short, big and fat, jui-cy flies in my tum-my!

p

13

Yes, we can have some fun, you, me and ev-'ry-one, just danc-ing in the sun.

f

16

So, why not come and dance with me?

ff

32. Come, let's dance!

Flowing ♩ = 116

Count 4 bars

When you dance with a frog, it's al - ways a plea - sure. Then we'll sit on a log, eat - ing fat flies at our lei - sure! Yum!

33. The fly's reply Ode to a bullfrog!

Quickly ♩ = 104—120

Bright and brave, quick and a - gile, whizz - ing through the air.

Blue and green, fast and fear - less, buzz - ing ev - 'ry - where.

Big and fat, mean and hun - gry, bull - frog looks at me. I'm

light and crisp, small and tas - ty . . . think I'd bet - ter flee! Buzz, whee!

34. Light of the moon

Gently ♩ = 72

Count 2 bars

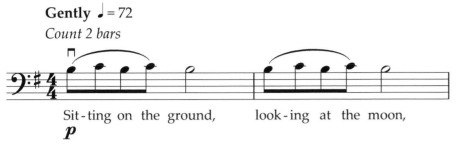

Sit-ting on the ground,   look-ing at the moon,
p

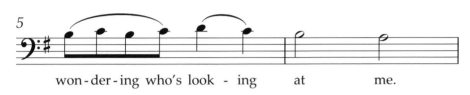

won-der-ing who's look - ing   at   me.

Won-der what they see,   look-ing down on me,   hope they see my beam-ing smile!

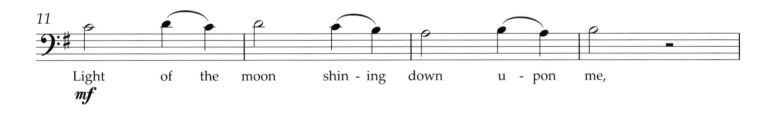

Light   of   the   moon   shin - ing   down   u - pon   me,
mf

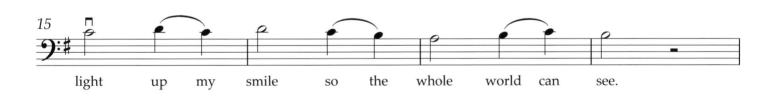

light   up   my   smile   so   the   whole   world   can   see.

Smil-ing at the moon,   wish-ing you were here,   light-ing up the world with me.
p

35. Thinking back

36. A dance for Dorian

Wistfully ♩ = 84—92

Count 2 bars

Do - ri - an mi - nor's a ve - ry sad key,

p

try not to cry as you play it to me.

f

Fall - ing from high notes the mu - sic des - cends,

down to the to - nic, that's where it ends.

p

© 2022 by Faber Music Ltd.

37. Side by side

Smoothly ♩ = 66

Count 2 bars

p

cresc.

f ———— *p*

© 2022 by Faber Music Ltd.

38. What to do?

Lively ♩ = 100—112
Count 2 bars

© 2022 by Faber Music Ltd.

39. Deep in the heart of the forest

Mysteriously ♩ = 69
Count 2 bars

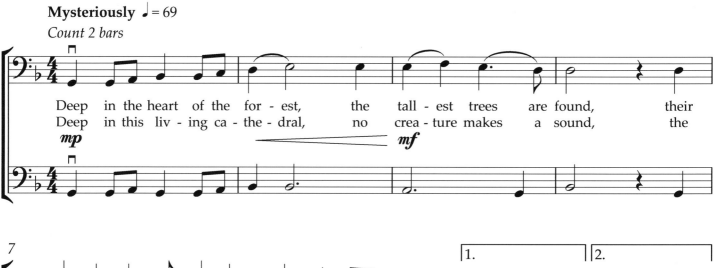

Deep in the heart of the for - est, the tall - est trees are found, their
Deep in this liv - ing ca - the - dral, no crea - ture makes a sound, the

branch - es spread so thick - ly that dark - ness cloaks the ground.
tall trees seem to ga - ther a cloak of si - lence round.

© 2022 by Faber Music Ltd.

40. Eggy soldiers!

Lazily ♩ = 84

Count 4 bars

Lyrics trad.

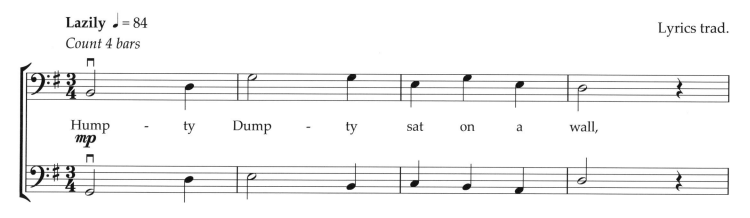

Hump - ty Dump - ty sat on a wall,

mp

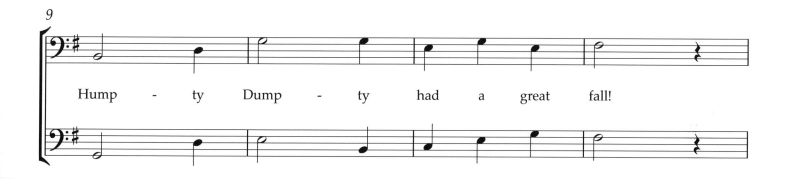

9

Hump - ty Dump - ty had a great fall!

13

All the king's hor - ses and all the king's men,

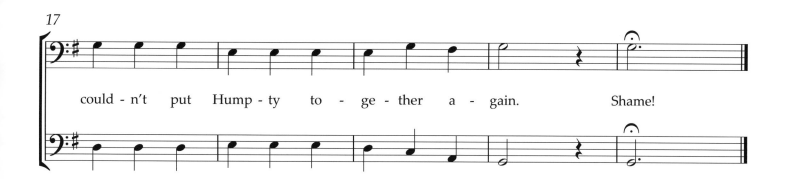

17

could - n't put Hump - ty to - ge - ther a - gain. Shame!

41. Let shine your light

Like a ballad ♩ = 80

Count 1 bar

42. Flying

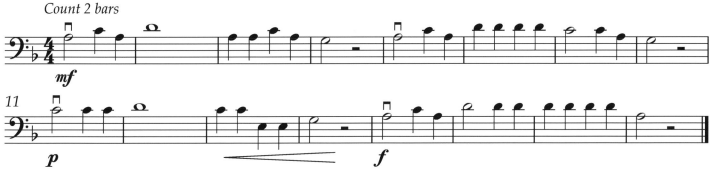

© 2022 by Faber Music Ltd.

43. Echo location

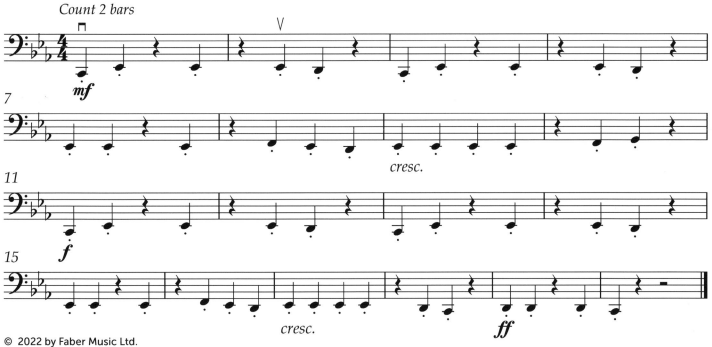

© 2022 by Faber Music Ltd.

44. Down in the dumps

Down in the dumps is how I might feel if I get my left hand fin-gers all wrong.
Down in the dumps is where I might be if I don't bow straight and so I look bad.

I must make sure they're in the right place; they must-n't be weak, but cer-tain and strong!
I must make sure my bow-ing is great, 'cause if it is not, then I'll feel quite sad.

© 2022 by Faber Music Ltd.

45. Little waltz

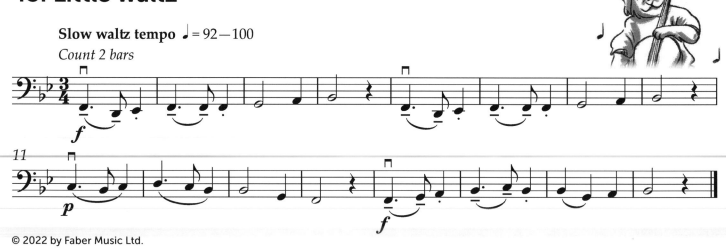

46. Far and near

47. Are you sure it's sharp?

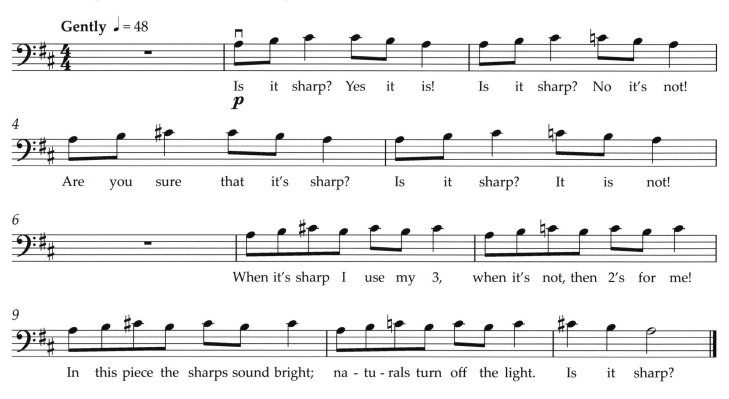

Is it sharp? Yes it is! Is it sharp? No it's not!

Are you sure that it's sharp? Is it sharp? It is not!

When it's sharp I use my 3, when it's not, then 2's for me!

In this piece the sharps sound bright; na - tu - rals turn off the light. Is it sharp?

48. Back and forth

With feeling ♩ = 63—72
Count 2 bars

All Fs are sharp in this song, Cs are not, so don't go wrong!

D string's where F sharps all stay, A string has no sharps to play.

49. Mini minuet

Dancing ♩ = 112—120
Count 4 bars

50. Spring into action

Lively ♩ = 84—92

51. Bowing free and easy

Hypnotic ♩ = 92

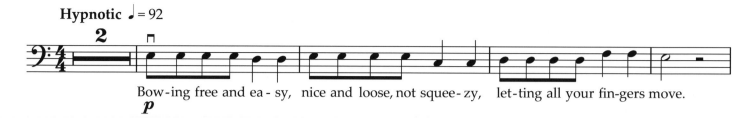

Bow-ing free and ea-sy, nice and loose, not squee-zy, let-ting all your fin-gers move.

Don't hold your bow tight-ly, just play ve-ry light-ly, then you'll make a sound so smooth.

Try to play quite near the fin-ger-board to hear the qui-et sound that suits this song.

Keep the mu-sic flow-ing with pre-ci-sion bow-ing, whe-ther notes are short or long.

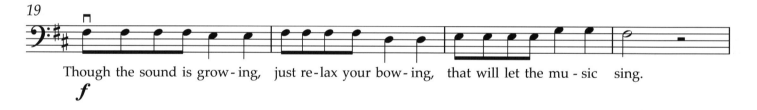

Though the sound is grow-ing, just re-lax your bow-ing, that will let the mu-sic sing.

Short notes need a small bow, long notes: let your arm go, then you'll get your sound to ring.

Some-thing else to men-tion: play-ing with-out ten-sion makes a per-fect bow-ing arm.

Bow-ing free and ea-sy, nice and loose, not squee-zy, that will work just like a charm!

52. Dot and Spot

53. Showtime!

Joyfully ♩ = 92

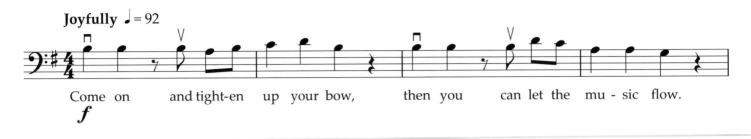

Come on and tight-en up your bow, then you can let the mu - sic flow.

f

Make sure your strings are all in tune, hur - ry, the con-cert's start - ing soon!

There are no emp-ty seats at all, we'll play to a packed con - cert hall, so take a

p

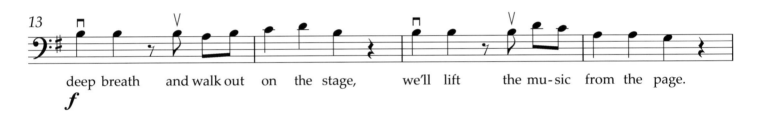

deep breath and walk out on the stage, we'll lift the mu - sic from the page.

f

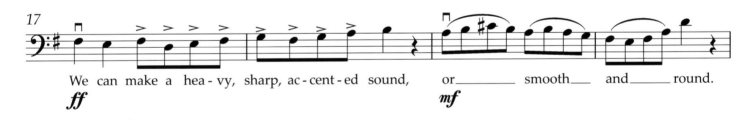

We can make a hea - vy, sharp, ac - cent - ed sound, or_____ smooth__ and_____ round.

ff   *mf*

Come on, let's go and make a start, mu - sic can move the hard - est heart.

f

When your bow flows a - cross the string, it is the most fan - tas - tic thing!

54. Twinkling waltz

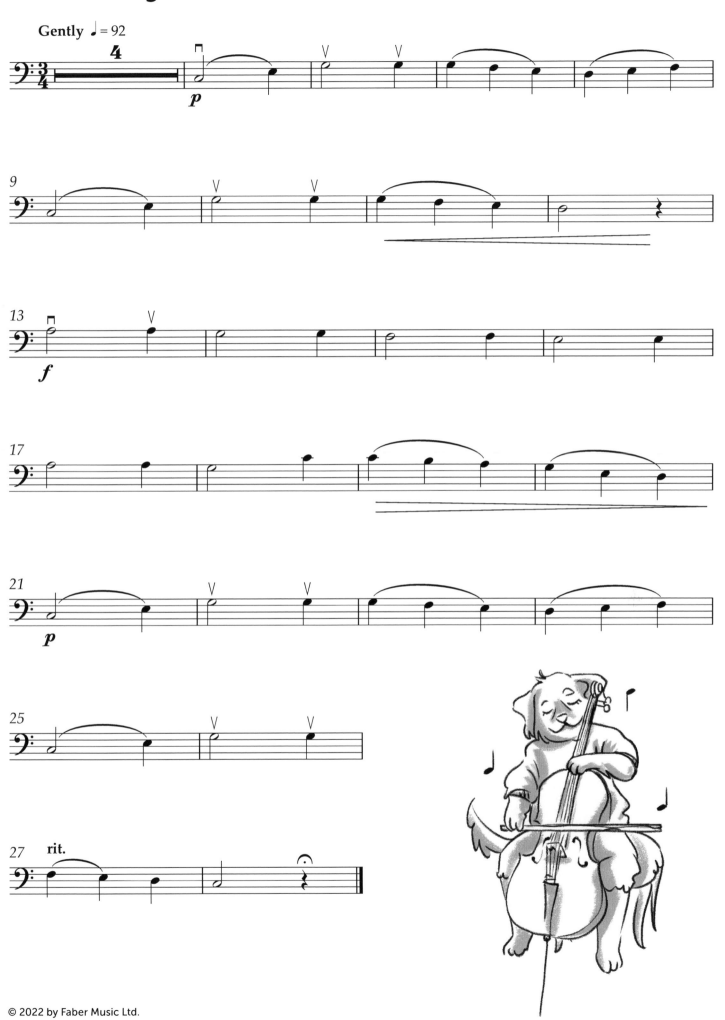

55. The pirates

Ya-ha-heartily! ♩ = 84

Ship - mates, all a - board! It's off to sea for you and me, a

chest of gold a - waits for those who show no fear!

We'll ex - plore be - yond the bow - ing straits and fin - ger falls, through

storm and thun - der, still we'll plun - der far and near! We

live as one 'cause it's such fun to

sail a - cross the o - cean blue with you and you and you and you! We'll

find the trea - sure, search - ing all a - round be - neath the ground, too

rich to mea - sure, friends, we'll live a life of cheer!

Bad bow hold? You'll walk the plank, 'cause there's no

mer - cy us pi - rates show! Good bow hold? Off we go!

56. Early one morning

Sadly ♩ = 60

Lyrics trad.

57. Worm dance

With drive ♩ = 100

It's so hard to dance when you're a worm! When you don't have legs, you tend to squirm!

f

I'm a big, jui-cy worm, crawl-ing all a-round. It's nice and cool where I live, un-der-ground!

f

In the soil, as I toil, I dream I'm a danc-er: if I ask "Can I dance?" care-ful how you

ans-wer! Just be kind and tell me how nice-ly I can dance.

p

Tell me that I'll be a star; please say there's a chance, so

squirm with me, twist with me, wrig-gle all a-round. It's hard to dance where I live, un-der-ground!

f

Stretch with me, squirm with me, wrig-gle on your bel-ly, just don't you stand on me with your great big

wel-ly, 'cause it's tough to be a worm! When you don't have legs, you tend to

f *f*

squirm! Danc-ing's ve-ry hard when you're a worm!

f *ff*